THE
Lord's prayer
JOURNAL

DR. DERWIN L. GRAY

THE
Lord's
prayer
JOURNAL

B&H
PUBLISHING
NASHVILLE, TENNESSEE

Cover design by B&H Publishing Group. Abstract art by korkeng/shutterstock.
Author photo by Transformation Church.

Published in association with The Bindery Agency, www.TheBinderyAgency.com.

1 2 3 4 5 6 7 8 • 25 24 23 22 21

Section 1

Our Father in heaven . . .

Use this QR code to see
Pastor Derwin Gray teach on this
section of the Lord's Prayer.

**YOU WERE
CREATED *BY* DIVINE
PURPOSE *FOR* A
DIVINE PURPOSE.**

**OUR ABBA
IS NOT A
DEADBEAT DAD.**

Section 2

Your name be honored as holy . . .

Use this QR code to see
Pastor Derwin Gray teach on this
section of the Lord's Prayer.

**WORSHIP IS SIMPLY
A LIFE LIVED IN
APPRECIATION OF
GOD'S MERCY. A
PRAYERFUL LIFE IS A
WORSHIPFUL LIFE.**

**GOD INVITES
US TO SHARE
IN HIS
HOLINESS.**

Section 3

Your kingdom come, your will be done,
on earth as it is in heaven . . .

Use this QR code to see
Pastor Derwin Gray teach on this
section of the Lord's Prayer.

WHEN YOU PRAY THE LORD'S PRAYER, YOU ARE PRAYING TO *KNOW* THE KING, TO ENTER AND *PARTICIPATE* IN THE KINGDOM, AND TO BE *TRANSFORMED* INTO THE IMAGE OF THE SON.

THE KINGDOM OF
GOD IS A KINGDOM
OF JUSTICE.

Give us today our daily bread . . .

Use this QR code to see
Pastor Derwin Gray teach on this
section of the Lord's Prayer.

WHEN WE PRAY, "GIVE US TODAY OUR DAILY BREAD" (MATT. 6:11), WE ARE MAKING A DECLARATION OF WORSHIP. WE ARE SAYING, "TODAY, WE TRUST YOU ABBA TO PROVIDE FOR US THROUGH CHRIST JESUS."

THE ONLY THING
WORRY DOES IS
SUCK THE ENERGY
OUT OF TODAY AND
DISTRACT US FROM
GOD'S PROMISES.

Section 5

*Forgive us our debts, as we also
have forgiven our debtors . . .*

Use this QR code to see
Pastor Derwin Gray teach on this
section of the Lord's Prayer.

**ANY POWER THAT
IS UNFORGIVING IS
NOT THE POWER OF
ABBA. IT IS FROM
THE FATHER OF
LIES, THE EVIL ONE.**

**LIVING WITH
UNFORGIVENESS
TAKES A PHYSICAL
AND SPIRITUAL TOIL.**

Section 6

Do not bring us into temptation,
but deliver us from the evil one.

Use this QR code to see
Pastor Derwin Gray teach on this
section of the Lord's Prayer.

DARK POWERS DESIRE TO ISOLATE AND SEPARATE US FROM THE HERD, OUR BROTHERS AND SISTERS IN CHRIST. IN CHRIST, WE PROTECT AND STRENGTHEN EACH OTHER.

JESUS OVERCOMES
THE TEMPTATIONS
OF THE DARK ONE.
BY INCORPORATION
INTO HIS LIFE AND
STORY, WE ARE
EMPOWERED BY HIM
TO DO THE SAME.

Discover the prayer God always answers

Also available from **DERWIN GRAY**

Through the pages of this book, pastor and bestselling author Derwin Gray will journey with you, in learning and living the prayer that God always answers. This prayer is commonly called the Lord's Prayer (Matt. 6:9-13).
The Lord's Prayer is the firm foundation God uses to build our lives on the Rock. It will help you break through to a completely new and refreshing prayer life.

GO DEEPER AS YOU JOURNAL!